WAYS OF BEING

WAYS OF BEING

SATI MOOKHERJEE

MoonPath Press
Sally Albiso
Award Winner

Poetry
ISBN 978-1-936657-74-2
LCCN 2022923746

Cover photo of Padilla Bay by Frank James

Author photo by Hannah Feller

Book design by Tonya Namura,
using Skolar Sans Latin and Minion Pro

MoonPath Press, an imprint of Concrete Wolf Poetry Series,
is dedicated to publishing the finest poets
living in the U.S. Pacific Northwest.

MoonPath Press
PO Box 445
Tillamook, OR 97141

MoonPathPress@gmail.com

http://MoonPathPress.com

for my friends, near
and nearer
in all your ways of being

Yes, who am I without you?
Just a philosopher, like everyone else.
— Czeslaw Milosz,
"My Faithful Mother Tongue,"
translated by Robert Pinsky

TABLE OF CONTENTS

TABLE OF CONTENTS

WAYS OF BEING

I. THE GREAT LUNG OF BAY

If you lived here, you'd be home already

The great lung of bay filled overnight, gurgitating, refluxing
as I slept, now is empty again,
shining entrails of green slime and ink-white mucoid streaks
attest that something was there recently, left.
This morning the cove is only a muddy field,
I'm at its excoriated edge, in a soft nibbling rain
watching a hawk tossed by the wind, a warm wind
that shimmies the leaves of the birch, strokes my head.

The tissue of the cove bed is stuccoed
with shell and remnants of shell, muck and evidence
of loss of life. The waters are away
around the bend, I can make out the twitching front,
at once something that was, and is still to come,
skewing, trailing, leading, lagging, dragging fingers
over the face of the tidal bed.

Everything falls through after a lifetime of holding
gestures—the hand cupping or fisted
or outstretched. A body slips out of another,

as in birth, or into another, as in sex. I watch: a body feeding.

A body flying. A body being eaten.
Eat, drink, merry-make. The sun comes and goes
and we privilege bright days over dark days,
the accompanied aria over the hoarse rooster's shouts

—we dress up, wash our hair, poke wires through holes
in flesh and dangle small shining stones from our heads,
hit our hands together
    when the song ends, to indicate pleasure.

Here's an ode to elisions, the occluded, the sun wadded
behind the gliding cloud,
    how very cold it is when that happens,
and how that chill can be so sweet, everything as it is:
emptied bay, sink of decay, vivid ribbons
of seaweed, the named birds crowded in the bramble
and, somewhere else, surely, birds still unnamed.
The catkins lie as they fall. The lawn studded

with dandelions who insist on living.
A bulbed ant goes about its business, around
the catkins' woolly cursive. Behind me one being calls
to another being.

The water is alive, still very far away. Sea air, a tonic
to cure what ails me, or perhaps just palliative.
    Mornings, I insist
on something hot to drink, at least to hold.
Every single shell before me once housed a body
that had its own way of being, preferences.
The cove bed is a battered metal sheet, scarred

as if by encaustics. A shore bird picks
at something. Red chair, rain-wet. Hummingbird, finally

stilling. Nectar in its mouth, briefly,
then a hunger for more nectar. There's always a tremor,
if you can feel it, the margins that wrap us
are not fixed, not the space between stillness and motion,
in which we think about moving, not
the vertical distance between the bird's body
and the sea, not our social distancing:
whom we embraced and whom we didn't.

What becomes important, very important: the ache
in the back. The clicking knee. The eyeball's
bulge of vitreous jelly. What we realize belatedly
was of great import: the chemistry of the birch tree, the sink
of bay between fillings, the way this cavity empties

and brims, lurches from thirst to drowning.

*

Bodies of birds, wind instruments not unlike
oboes. The interval between the earth's body,
mine. The way I look to the landscape,
seascape. My indrawn breath.

The soughing inside the stand of trees.
The crushed carapace and the soft meaty meaning.

The arrow indicating the one-way street. I am back
to believing the past is as real as anything,
and I might as well live there. I am, you might say,
divorced from reality, but I was married to reality
once upon a time. Reality is my ex,
I have consciously uncoupled. The tide
is constantly arriving, but also

not arriving, the waves just riffing
on a larger theme. A kind of insistence all about me:
a row of birds, all with something to say. A pickup rounds
the bend, announcing itself, guttural and polluting.
Microeconomies of grasses: distributed seeds
and plain flowerings,

organic matter thick and granular over the flats.
Out of the clutter of squeaks and chittering
    one voice arises,
falls silent, then another voice arises.
The birds, like me, only have a handful of things
to say, like me, they say them over and over again.
There is no other way to fill a life. Still the water nears,
a shallow front, shimmering in the middle distance.

Another voice pings, like a bell at a train crossing.
Something approaches. The water is pale blue, almost white.
I am preoccupied with symptoms, pockmarks
and fine prints in mud, busted shells. I am waiting,
writing letters, saying this is how it is, this is how it was,

this how it might be. And: I miss you.
And: I have loved loving you. I set the words down
each next to next,
        thinking they will find each other like wound edges
healing by secondary intent. The body gives out, in the end,
under hazel skies, beside streaming rills
and fronts, and in midst of "consciousness."

I wonder if I've crossed over to a place I can't return from.
I make myself look away from the naked, teeming cove bed,
toward the house, a glass of water, yellow
and cloudy with apple cider vinegar, on the sill.
I live here, I see that now, and that must mean I'm home.

II. SITTING BY THE SEA

II. SITTING BY THE SEA

Brut

In hour one of sitting, tide hemmed the bulkhead.

In hour two, the muddy underskirt exposed.

In hour three, gulls came to feed, second winter

juveniles, mostly. I cast

the pock-pocking of shells

they downthrew against rock,

the tocking of some soft clock, understood in hour six

my conceit was the time of death

for the being lifted out of the sea,

flung through air, exposed, rent,

the undefended body and the sharp beak.

In hour seven, a roar, like a mobbing crowd,

swelling into hour eight: widgeons

unseen across the blinkered cove.

Late in the night—hour ten? eleven?

a mesh bag of oysters

washed up on my beach,

and I set them in a pail of sea water.

Night vaulted over itself like a wave,

the stuttered rain

of falling shells commenced again the next day,

hour eight came round again and I shucked

and ate and shucked and ate

and shucked and ate, sent them sloshing

down my gullet with a cheap can of brut, sparkling.

Feather

for Oren Traub

Kelp binds the driftwood stub, like rusty wire.
The sea streams this way.
Smell of mildew. Drunken jigging in an alley.
A cedar box of keys.
Somewhere important things are still locked up,
or have been released?
Or are no longer important? You have so many keys.
The self swells like a wave, crests
like a wave, is diminished, backs down
to nothing. The sea streams that way.
You can't help yourself, you ascribe tenderness
to the way the seaweed holds the driftwood twist.
A schoolgirl pauses in an alley
to pose flamboyantly,
miniskirt, thigh, stocking, his sheepish smile,
her monkey grin,
his arm around her waist. Shoebox
of photographs in a keyed fire safe,
boxes constructed in space, and holding space.
You can't help yourself: wind animates
a molted feather and you read the waving feather
as another way of being.

Cross Purposes

Hills placid as dromedaries around the slouching sea.
Wool lap blanket, red squares and blue squares.
Smoke fogged the room and made it difficult
to breathe: Marlboro. Camel. You were so small,

at the beginning of everything. Now: wood smoke,
weed smoke, sweet and spicy. Peppery scent of peonies,
once so small: newborn violet shoots
wet-looking, ruffled as labia, pink as raw meat.

You lift your eyes to the buzz cut hilltops.
Set at the perpendicular: mountain and ocean, pilings
pinning fixed spots in the sharp flowing sea.
What you want more than anything abuts

what you need more than anything,
at cross purposes, you locate your self
at the intersection of axes running back to the past
and toward the future, pulling away from each other

at any rate. Hills rise, shaved or shaggy,
the sea slinks, and in the sky, the bodies of birds
free-fall in crisscross shapes.

Twist

Two clouds become one cloud. What was defined
became indistinct. What was differentiated
was absorbed. The sea kept lisping
in my left ear. My right ear was hot from the sun.
Tides of cold air crossed my face.
I remembered the clouds as they had been.
As you were! Would that I could be.

Repair

This morning the seaside soundscape
is trammeled by the din of heavy machinery,
high-pitched and high-decibel, metal
    doing something violent to metal.
Maritime industry didn't get the memo that it ought defer

to tender artistic sensitivities. Someone is repairing something,
boat engine, machine designed to carry
some thing or some body from one place
to another place. I am covering paper with words,

secreting chemicals over the dried pulp of dead trees
because I am evidently also in the engine repair business,
bettering the vehicle that carries me from here
    to somewhere else,
delivers me to a landscape where I have not been before,

or returns me to where I am supposed to be.

Sunset

Welted sky above a bruise-colored sea, weal
and stripe, the cool hand of night
cannot come soon enough

to stop the burning. I wait. Black sky, finally.
Clouds like gauze bandages, a small cool moon.
The stars rise like a rash, nodular.

The ocean is no longer visible, only sensed:
lung, respiring in clear gases that rise
wet. Goose-pimpled sky. White-hot bowl of fire

at my feet. How good the burnt sky won't scar,
bunting-blue every morning,
even as now it is pricked and asterisked

with cell tower and wing lights, satellites scratching
paths in the atmosphere. *Bring this home*,
I hear myself think, but I can't understand

what my mind is trying to tell me.
My blood loops in closed paths. I lean back,
let the voices around me corrode into sound

without meaning, as the snapping fire,

as the faraway barking dog. I think some more about repair,

renewal after violence, I lie, I self-soothe.

III. TERRARIUM

for Shannon

Ground

Lay your warm body on the warm earth
and sense how deep the roots go, the roots

we can't see, think of the acres
of hot black lightless matter under your body.

I think the past is a perfectly fine place to live.
Why not be native to it, visit the present

as necessary, a tourist, in transit, on a brief journey.
I can see you're dying. This terrarium,

even with its carefully laid nests of leaves and grass
and twigs, can't keep you, I don't want to keep you,

go home, back to where you need to be.

Bird on a Piling

Dear Cyan, the morning after your mother
lay you down in fistfuls in the ice water sea,
she came to sit with me.

She told me how the sea started to roil, went from placid
to activated, the tide getting a little, well, aggressive—
your mother said "I know it had nothing to do with anything,
it was a wake, or a weather system thing."
"Of course," I agreed.

Where we sat was unpleasant, Cy, the sun too loud,
the air too cold, almost abrasive. The waves kept coming,
which is a stupid thing to say, but I felt
I needed them to let up a bit, it was too much.

We could not understand how the bird on the piling
withstood the slicing wind. How it sat there as long as we did.
Was the sitting purposeful? Or without purpose?

Your mother observed the water was the color
of your name. She didn't feel the cold,
even as I had chemical warming pouches stuffed

in my socks, wore lined boots, two pairs of pants,
a swaddled hot water bottle against my chest,

24

two down jackets, a blanket. I held a mug of hot tomato soup.
Still I shook with cold, flinching under the sun.

I said of the bird: "What a strange place to choose to be."
Your mother only nodded, said nothing.

>

I ask you why we do not Sense as fully
in the cereal aisle of the community food cooperative
as on the shore.

I think it's a good question.
Perhaps the fault lies with the Sensor
and not the Sensee.

I ask why we Sense less acutely
in the lube shop
than on the mountain top.

I suggest my belief
is a flimsy thing, that it doesn't hold up
much, that it's scenic beauty

doing the heavy lifting.
I suggest that the Sensor
is perhaps less bodied

in circumstances that are expansive
and where there is movement, like
sleek mudflats emerging as the tide recedes,

flocks of plovers

showing us how they slip

across worlds: the liquid slough,

mown field, cloth sky,

not minding boundaries.

I suggest that to at once be lesser than,

to take up less space,

and, at the same time

to be in the presence of other beings

who move freely and with purpose, or not,

or gracefully, or not,

enables a different kind of sensing.

I could go on, and I do. I say that the cereal aisle

is largely static, that the boxes don't move,

and ergo don't remind us that nothing stays

the same. But then I see you are not here,

where oil stains a concrete floor, men with black

fingertips ask if you have a coupon

you'd like to use today.

I realize later,

the more important question is how

do you walk the cereal aisle of the coop

when there is no one to buy cereal for?

How do we walk aisles of the ordinary, having lost

what we have lost, or knowing

what we might lose? How do we make it,

how are we to want to make it,

want to make Sense, or even just sense,

of any of this, even as we sit side by side and watch

birds cross the white field of sky,

larvae in their throats

larvae left behind

writhing in the brackish shallows of the slough.

Fantasie on a Theme of Violence

1.

Empty stretches of sleep, then swells: inchoate cries,
a woman's voice, asking for something. Then ebb tide.
Silent black mudflats where the dream had just roiled.

2.

She walks down a corridor, gaze fixed ahead. Her
hand strokes the closed faces: wall, frame, door, frame.
Then wall again.

3.

She washes her feet, her hands in the courtyard. An
attendant wipes them dry. He weeps. She weeps too, or
does she? He opens the small side gate to the cove.

4.

Lunar noon, three moons stacked like a cairn, one
white stone atop the next. Golden sky, gold sea. Anger
like a rogue wave, at such luminosity.

5.

Her hands are bones sleeved in skin, the nail beds
like bits of armor at the tips, little shields. She stares at
the sea.

6.

No, no, no.

Willful. Headstrong. Insolent.

7.

The sleek skin of the water peckles with bubbles. A slick black head appears at the surface. Seal? It comes closer. Emissary. It bows and recedes and the sea closes back over it like a membrane. She shuts her eyes.

8.

One waits for something to begin or for something to end. She waits every day, for no one and for nothing.

9.

Once there had been beginnings, a girlhood spent beside a river banked in red clay and flanked by fertile fields. But her childhood had not been happy. Her mother, in her own childhood, had heard of a village where white columns studded the fields and paths, every man, woman, and child ossified in their own bodies.

10.

She remembers the unwatered plants in the courtyard that morning parched and drooping. *Careless.* She had opened the door. The bed was empty, the swirl of bed sheets seemed carved from marble, smooth as statuary.

One hair on the cloth of the pillow, rising and falling like a line on canvas.

Later, she would wind it around her finger like a ring.

11.

A tear in the sea. The black head birthed again.

12.

The emissary swam closer, neared the frilled skirt of shore. Her body twisted in the clear water, hair braided like rope. She surfaced, her dorsal half exposed, belly in the shoals.

13.

She kept the windows and doors to that room tightly sealed, trying to bottle that scent like attar. But already it was changing.

And the bright ring had dulled to string.

14.

Hail began to fall in hard little moons on her back, her palms. The emissary reared out of the froth, and the water streamed down her body, the green-white of new spring wood, stringed with muscle.

15.

Laughter, insouciant. At such a moment. *Rude—*
before she could stop the thought.

16.

The emissary turned and dove into the water,
raucous and ungraceful. The sea flared up, gas-yellow
flame, then swallowed her body.

17.

Her wrists hurt. Bone-white casings had formed, soft
cuffs of cartilage. She peeled them off before they set. The
skin underneath was raw and oozing.

The sea was already completely still, not moving even
a little bit.

18.

She rose, left the shore. The manservant opened the
gate soundlessly. The polished moons hung in the sky
behind her. The canopy overhead teemed with vivid blue
parakeets, screaming.

Wood and Wool

1.

You are wood, you are wool,

you are the intricate skeleton of the desiccated leaf,

of the dead, dehydrated papyrus-bloom.

2.

You are simple as a scroll of birch shaving.

3.

That's neither here nor there.

But, no such thing. Unless

there is some other place in between.

4.

You are lymph, you are fascia

and the soft unbounded places.

5.

There, there, don't cry.

Here, here. Cry.

Sow clear seed, a saline-rinse

baptism of your new countenance.

6.

You sit by the sea. You are wool, you are wood.
Rainwater beads on your body, freshwater pearls
on your jacket, but saltwater soaks in, is absorbed.

I think you are third-spacing.
Rain water inserts itself into sea water.
Don't know about the other world,

but this one keeps time, the softly ticking rain,
tidal recessions and spillings forward, the absences
and presences, and in-betweens, I know you don't live here

anymore, and you don't live there,
there, there, my friend,
you are wood, you are wool, you are the tocking
of your heart against the mattress.

This Age

Grassé-matinées, rumpled t-shirt dresses, sitting in the sun,
coffee soaked with Baileys for no reason or occasion at all.
Those were then. Now: a *grassé-soirée*: evening fat
with porch sitting, sky freckled with stars,
a house across the street spitting arcs of ember
from its chimney. Dogstar magnolia stars the nearer sky.
A vase of daffodils, euphorbia,
          and some sort of spiky, cork-screwy grass.
The jelly jars throb with tea candle flame and we pretend
that to mark this birthday is sane.

To be fair, there is real laughter
          when you conjure the sideways ponytail,
the imaginary friends, their mouthiness,
          their Birmingham accents.
The flowers are too pretty.
Completely out of place. From a different age,
for a different age. Someone vanishes and someone else
opens her eyes every morning,
goes to the chair by the window,
          dips the brush in black watercolor
and fills a square page, stroke, stroke, stroke, *la page grassée,*
soaked in paint, bulging and glossy with emptiness.

Each Day

Three days after, Jim and I walked in the woods,
a traverse trail, such that near the end
the trees thinned and the land fell sharply away,
and there was the Salish Sea, dolloped
with islands, each haloed it seemed, ringed
in blue-green. At the top, we saw a shard
of float-glass lake through trees
and, at that, turned at once to walk back down,
as if we had only come all that way to confirm
the lake still existed.

*

Halfway down-mountain, we heard birdsong,
something brushed and fluttery. I thought it a wren maybe.
Jim stopped, pointed. "There," he said, "Do you see it?"
I looked and looked, but couldn't see the bird,
though the song continued, tremolo, sweet.
He kept pointing. "There. Right there."

There was no bird. The trunk of a fir rubbed
against a dead trunk, both rising out of the same stump.
The singing came from the place where they met,
a dead tree, and a living tree leaning against it.

*

People ask me about you. I stop myself
from saying "Can't you tell she died last Tuesday?"

*

The cruel morning keeps coming for you, relentless.
The sun persists, though I know you wish it didn't.
And I look, each day, my friend,
     for a bird that will never exist,
and I hear the strange soft song it makes.

IV. PLACES I'VE BEEN

Places I've Been

Mudflats, streaked by fringes of residual tide.
In the tall grass, a charm bracelet, forgotten.

Above the tree line, the air was so much colder,
and the forest became a red meadow

of some tough-leafed plant I didn't know
the name of. I was alone there,

for some time.
Many minutes later, the children appeared.

Smeared window glass.
Smeared sky, glob of sun approaching a striate sea.

Cream cheese on apple slices. Sunlight like a palm
on my face. Boulder-studded fields, gorse at the edges.

I moved inside something, and through it,
bevel tip slipping into skin, then the wall of the vein.

I was alone in a stony field,
surrounded by myths, and stories of hardship.

Little popping sounds in the hedgerows.

Is that true? Did that happen? Golden cliffs.
Alpine blueberries. The children move out of sight again.

Hut

No sounds of water licking rock.
Yes, jabbering birds. Yes, lanes in the dry sky,

that corridor of air yours,
and this one mine. A strain along the muscle

of my phantom wing.
The birds are dirt-bathing.

Thirst golden at the back of my throat.
The back of my neck dirty,

dust over the dorsal surfaces of my feet. This shelter
barely that, a dwelling,

a place to rest, and wonder
at how moisture's held in the atmosphere.

We can't perceive it, but it's there,
in the slick of a feather of a bird's back,

the shine of the white of an eye,
yours or mine, at the center of things

that are alive. It has to be.

What Bangkok will Always Mean

Bleary-eyed arrivals in the dead of night.
Dome of rice, crusty cutlet of whitefish
stamped with a polka dot of lime.
An etching titled "Zeppelin" on the wall.
The next morning, fruits in jeweled
gelatinous abundance. A view of the railway station's
commuter trains and street sweepers.
Watching people I knew I'd never see again
step into their days, the slick of their freshly
washed and combed heads, their cinched
school bags and clenched briefcases.
Smoke-colored morning sky. Thick sheets
of glass between the sky-bridge of the airport hotel
and the train platform, rendering their lives,
mine, mute and unknowable.

One Subject

My notebook is labeled "One Subject," and I think,
that's right, how did you know?
One subject. Everything else is object.
But—also one objective.
One kingdom. One capricious sovereign.
One commonwealth of fear, of aspiration.
So many verbs. So much doing.

One subject trying to live in "good relations,"
trying to remember "everyone has a journey,"
trying to remember "I have a journey,"
trying to understand what that means
when all I ever seem to want
is things as they used to be.

Refreshing

Fresh bruise, *green-yellow*, or *spring green*,
the paper-sleeved crayon's particularity,
this field daffodil-colored bloom on my thigh resurrects
the scent of that waxy stick.
That was me in the flower-print miniskirt
one *yellow-green* spring, one noon
by the fountain at Piccadilly Circus.
How the flighty have sunk! This bruise a lovely
surprise—evoking "young," evoking
the earthy scent of daffodils,
the hope of the fresh crayon's smooth sculpted tip,
the hundreds of petals I drew, lacy or scallop or sharp,
hub-and-spoke suns, before the crayon
dulled to stub, the painstaking process of peeling back,
to render the useless useful again, peeling back,
the reset, the refresh, the keep going,
the try again, bits of paper detritus
littering the tables where I summoned blooms and orbs,
and crumbs of wax the color of spring dirtied
the corners of my fingernails.

V. EXPRESSIONS & VOCABULARIES

Flashcard: *L'Exigence*

There are some mornings you slip so easily
under the skin of the day, you step
into the world an agent, *avec fortitude.*
Grâce à toi, grâce à moi, grâce à toute.
You remember other times you felt that way,
afternoons, years ago, in a city chalked
in pastels. A magpie danced on a skinny ledge,
and when your hands came off the window bars,
soot powdered your palms and finger tips.
Evenings were too hot to be indoors,
and you lay on a reed mat on the roof
and watched Soviet satellites stream overhead.
There was a face in the broken window
of the unlit house across the courtyard,
or there wasn't. Either way,
you felt adequately contained
by the world, you fit, or it fit, *la taille,*
and *la tasse* of tea was perfectly sized for your hand,
and beautiful words fit in your mouth,
alongside the bitter sand of leaf grounds,
sugar sludge, crystals you'd split
finer still between the ridged edges
of your front teeth. Yes, some days
you wore the world, you were clad.
L'exigence, then, was to step in the striped river,

and to move at the rate the river moved,

what was meant to be fixed

stayed fixed—*mise en place*—the boulder,

the trestle, the fronting red clay path—

and the rest of it streamed—green fish,

the fallen boat-shaped leaf—

along with you, you went streaming.

There was your intention, the river's intention,

and they were one and the same,

there was the fragrance of the garbage heap,

kites stamping the sky, there was a caucus

of crows that convened, dissipated,

everything moved as you perceived it as moving,

your spit tasted sweet, the wax in your ears

softened to unguent from the heat, you yourself

moved with the smoothness of the clock's minute hand,

that was the only law, that you move as intended.

Conjugation with Venn Diagram

The Self and the Other, Jim Coan

1.

Tu me manques, you are missing
to me. I lack you. The subject

is the person missing, as in gone.
I am the object, the one who misses.

Tu nous manques (tu manques à nous)
(You are missing to us) = We miss you.

2.

Self is the place
where the circle of you

overlaps the circle of me, self
is a gibbous moon.

I am constant and always full.
And my self hungers

and sates, waxes and wanes
as a moon seems to.

Mind The Gap!

Oh, believe me, I do.
I mind the crack, the maw, the hole in the sock,
and the defect in the shoe. The pocket of gum
the tartar sticks to. Between grasp
and reach, between this shiny object
and that dull thing, between gravitas and gaudy
wing. Between segura cactus and salty sea.
Within me. Between my various internal densities,
the things I'm convinced of and the things I think.
And the things I think I ought
to believe. But don't believe, not truly. The gap
between what you want and what I want
you to want. Oh my love, my sweet: Please.
Go on, don't mind me.

Stress Timed

Ours is a stress-timed language,
all things emphatically not equal,

we linger on some syllables and hop-skip others,
there is the matter of schwa,

that featureless space, that faceless uh,
that   ,

like like like embolalia,
how amazing to jaw

the bone up and down, tap the tongue
to the teeth, litter the air

with noises. The slumping candle strobes
annoyingly, clamoring birds tear apart

a half-dead animal,
my words stutter-step like

what's not to like, plosives in my mouth,
small hollows form and unform, vowels

like stem cells, I'm all like quavering
like a tympanic membrane, like

stressed, pressed, lingering over
what lingers, obsessed,

astonished at the half-lives, the staying power
of my animal sounds.

Present

Well that's neither here nor there.

Not here? Fine, but to be so sure of what is there,
or not there…I think you're lying.

The horizon is only one seam among many
that join this to there.

Cast iron bird on the shelf, a present. It offends,
seems a perversity: lightness, motion, expressivity

rendered inert and utterly silent. Unless
it's an icon of contracture?
    As I must first imagine my body

ossified to stick, to splint, so that later it will release
fully in corpse pose—legs falling open, mouth slack

and gaping even as no words should emerge.
Must I live here, utterly?

What relief, to lift my eyes to the hills,
to the topography of immense clouds,

to watch them evolve, those great masses
the size of human settlements.

The birdness of this art piece eludes, frankly.
There's cloud cover, clouds sliding over and through

one another, and here's flitting paralyzed me.

VI. WAYS OF BEING

Cage

I suppose to render a bird in cast iron is no sillier
than trapping it in a poem,
    although there's an exculpatory

complexity in these kinked inked markings,
paper itself the body of a tree, a perch,

the turned page makes a microbreeze,
and the poem takes wing in the breath, or in the airspace

between eye and screen. A flicker
outside my window has been steadily drilling.

Maybe she would concur with the medium's aptness,
were she interested in the politics of concurrence,

see in the cast iron her essential self—something hard,
to be wielded. Leave soft and fluffy to juncos

and wrens. She is a headbanger, less kin
to flute and more to jackhammer…The flicker is gone,

or gone quiet. The poem falls silent. To cage
a poem in the head of a bird, perverse.

China

Tea roses on bone china, tildes of tendril
and leaf, fine gold banding. Some days, things are lovely,
a fringed shoreline, inlaid with firths and coves
and lakes. Other days, everything speaks to
violence—the forces that broke underlying structures,
cracked canyons—floods and tectonics
to which metaphor has no relevance. What happened
happened. The pretty saucer, the ground-up bodies
of all those animals separated from their souls.
Some days, the tea roses are old blood stains on
threadbare bedsheets, some days, brown-sugar blooms.

...Or How I Learned to Stop Worrying and Love

the veil, the muzzle, the snood, in the later days I grew
accustomed to being inside a kind of room
that I carried through the outer room of the world.
I was self-contained, my breaths were warm.
I didn't speak unless I really felt like it
and I never felt like it. I crossed the street if I saw
anyone coming, and if my glasses fogged,
    so much the better.
I pulled the hat low, played the child's dubious
hide and seek: if I could not see you,
    you could not see me.
And when the double-masking days began
—well, a kind of ecstasy. My mind was at rest,
could attend, undistracted. No mouths but on screens,
no fleshy holes opening and closing. No wet edges
of lip or naked teeth. I took to lining the rims
of my upper and lower eyelids in black pencil
to be more narrow, more severe, to further disguise,
a faceless device, and that was another way of being.

Investment

Morning as real estate, attention mortgaged against time,
I think: *interest*, I think: *cap rate*, I wonder how do I make
the most of this? Residual darkness in the folds

of the rhododendron's scaly buds, as if night were bluing
in wash water, everything emerging clean.
In these woods, a hip-licking sea
of ferns so green they're blue, breaking against trees fixed

in arrested postures of outreach, a study in horizontals,
the firs toil not, nor do they spin,

they reach without intent to grasp. To take up space
to take up space. That is another way to be.

This precious perishing morning. Scarcity of resource.
Realized gain. Unrealized gain. Realized
losses. The ferns, as a body, navy-blue

the forest floor, in the late afternoon sunlight will
cross the air like beams, scaffolding. *Margin*,
what time I can afford to spend, and what I may keep,

what hours separate out, rise to the top of the quotidian
like cream. An exercise in accounting:

the strata of what's buried, sunk expenses,
what is receivable, will in-stream. That horizon. That margin,
the thin layer where we actually live. Hours straddle

hours, as living things climb
over and out of living things: saplings from nurse trees,
shelves of fungi, creamy and chewy, studding

tree trunks. Time, fertile and compounding, begets
time. Among thousands of outstretched arms, I wade,

I wade, through the frond-dark sea.

Freed

If the arm may not move here, or there,
it must imagine a new gesture, a radical movement.
The leg bent against itself, in *tendu*, may evolve:
piqué turn, *attitude*. And so it goes, the vine curlicues
along rigid scaffolding bamboo, the formal poem
says: no, not that word, not that word either, and knocks
the mind out of its usual loops

into a new field. The door locks and the cell
becomes the whole world, straitjacket straps
crisscross the thoracic cavity to shape
each newborn breath, the blinkered gaze is a tunnel,
a path, you cannot tell me where it ends. It doesn't end.
I'll tell you what it looks like when I get there, root-bound,
folded against myself, as I am, the way origami paper
is creased and doubled and bent into blooming.

Easier Done Than Said

Deer snout print on the glass where last night
some soul lingered, regarding me.
Stirrings in the dead blood grass.
    The last of the mustard greens.
The first of the Korean maples' salmon leaves.
I'll do what has to be done. Just don't want to talk about it.
Too many words in the world, in my head,
speckling every surface, aphids. I want things clean, emptied
—as in spaciousness, not loss. Swept or laundered or

cut back, whatever. Just: unsaid. Please, can we leave it,
can we be as the deer who watched me sleep,
then was done, walked off, hooves on the hard patio,
then in damp grass, musty flank glancing the fatsia's
tips, a series of small sounds that meant nothing,
stood for nothing, will be remembered by nobody.

Needs Must

The musk of warm rain on moss on rock,
ahead dapple-work meadow / lake / wood
then saltwater pleated into firths.
I guess I *needs must* stand atop the steaming rock,
feels like summer rain although it's only March,
the ground flushed from deep, hot through the soles
of my shoes, my arms, under my tuque.
An eagle settles in the tree. Names of islands.
Names of trees. European names laid over First names.
The heat from the old names still comes through.
It rises, softly. It *needs must* do. Like the heat
of my name from before I knew you.

This Human Need

To make things like other things, greedy
as a simile. Sea-colored clouds

and cloud-colored sea. A kind of twisting, reflexive
as a verb, bending the world

around the axis of self. *Se manquer*,
or *l'hitpallel*. To locate God

in the Locating. The yoga of worshiping your worst fears,
bhakti. Sky-colored tern. To perceive the sky

as the color of a bird. Do to yourself.
To note the stone-colored cloud. To note:

cloud-colored stone, wet with rain and tide-slapped.
To inventory, to measure: the neap's

skinny, gritty margin. The sprawling edges
of human settlements. To be regarded,

whether too big to be completely seen,
like the sky or the ocean,

or too small to be seen at all. To be unseen,

move too glacially to be perceived

as moving, or move too quickly, fast as an osprey,

seeing like an osprey sees: bending the world

around the axis of its body like

ACKNOWLEDGEMENTS

I am grateful for Sally Albiso's body of work and legacy, and honored to accept the Poetry Book Award given in her name.

A thousand thanks to John Davis, Sharon Hashimoto, Susan Landgraf, Arlene Naganawa, Robert McNamara, Michael Spence, Ann Spiers, and John Willson.

I am indebted to Shannon Paglia, Sara White, and Kirsten Barron who made room in the world for me to write this book.

Grateful acknowledgement is made to Frank James, physician and photographer, for the cover photograph of the Padilla Bay tidal flats—and for his unwavering dedication to the health and wellbeing of all of our people and communities.

"One Subject" is informed by the Fall 2020 online discussion between Dr. Tracy Bear, Dr. Paul Gareau, Faculty of Native Studies, and Dan Levy, as part of the University of Alberta's Indigenous Canada MOOC offering.

"Conjugation with Venn Diagram" is informed by "The Self and the Other," Jim Coan, in *The Virginia Quarterly Review*, 98/2, Summer 2022.

An earlier version of "Wood and Wool" appears in *Salamander*.

ABOUT THE AUTHOR

Sati Mookherjee is the author of *Eye* (Ravenna Press, 2022).
Her work appears in literary journals and anthologies
like *Comstock Review, Cream City Review*, and *Sonora
Review*. Her collaborations with contemporary classical
composers have been performed or recorded by ensemble
(The Esoterics, Contemporary Chambers and Players)
and solo musicians (Hope Wechkin: *Leaning Toward the
Fiddler*). Recipient of an Artist Trust/Washington State Arts
Commission Fellowship Award, Sati is a lifelong resident of
the Pacific Northwest.